Profile of an Entrepreneur

Ignite your Passion & Power of Why

Discover if a Home Business is Right for You

Linda Compton

Dedication

This primer is dedicated to those who sense that there is much more to life than they are currently experiencing; to those who want to live, grow and give more fully. It is for those considering the possibility of a viable home business solution for some of life's most pressing situations; or who are seeking greater meaning and a personal transformation. It is also for those who are looking for enhanced health, increased financial security, or perhaps more time or geographic freedom. It is my heart's desire that within these pages you will recognize what an exceptional opportunity awaits you; experience a sparkling sense of hope, and gain a glimpse of all that is possible and available to you. And that through your own process of discernment, you will discover whether or not a home business is right for you at this point in your life.

Milinda —
So grateful for our
friendship & very
glad to be connected
again.
♡ Beth

Milinda
Welcome to the
Team!
Blessings!

Profile of an Entrepreneur

Ignite your Passion & Power of Why

Discover if a Home Business is Right for You

Table of Contents

Acknowledgements

There are so many individuals who have informed, inspired and supported my personal growth. Trying to name them all would be folly. It is my hope that they know who they are, as I have tried to express my gratitude in many ways over the years, and continue to do so. However, here I do want to thank Mr. Don Green, Executive Director of the Napoleon Hill Foundation and Mr. Bob Proctor, from whom I continue to learn so much. I also want to acknowledge all the members of this remarkable, worldwide community of fellow entrepreneurs; especially the mentors and leaders who daily continue to challenge and encourage me. This is the headiest and most heart-warming enterprise I have ever had the privilege of pursuing. Finally, I want to thank my business partner and chapter contributor, Billi Grossman, RDN, who also helped me edit and format this book; as well as every other valued member of our wonderful Team. You inspire and energize me; and I am deeply grateful for the opportunity to make dreams – mine and those of so many others - come true.

Linda Compton

What successful entrepreneurs & thought leaders are saying about *Profile of an Entrepreneur*

"Linda has written an excellent book on the Profile of an Entrepreneur. Reading this little book will help you answer questions that might concern you if you have the desire to be an entrepreneur.

An entrepreneur is a special individual who is not determined by age, sex, or even the number of educational degrees one may have.

Follow the author chapter by chapter and you will have a great understanding of what is required to be successful.

I have been an entrepreneur since early childhood and I can assure you the information in Profile of an Entrepreneur will be a great help on your journey."

Don M. Green, Executive Director

Napoleon Hill Foundation
www.naphill.org

"A lot of great information packed into the pages of this small book. The reader is brought to self-examination as to what they want, why they want it and what they have to give to get there. Combining practical information on the network marketing industry along with soul searching questions, this book is something everyone should read as they venture into this industry for the first time, or if they are at a cross-roads in their career."

Jeannie Boniface – Success Through Focus & Fun! Network Marketing Leader, Motivational Speaker, Success Coach
http://www.JeannieBoniface.net

"Profile of an Entrepreneur, Ignite Your Passion & Power of Why by Linda Compton, is a well-written piece to assist you in evaluating whether or not a home based business it right for you.

Linda does a wonderful job of highlighting the basics of the network marketing profession. In doing so, she equips the reader with the right information to evaluate the profession as a whole and provides criteria to help you select the right company.

If you are looking to join a network marketing business or have just joined one, I recommend this book for you."

JJ Birden, Professional Network Marketer, Former NFL Football Player, Author of:
When Opportunity Knocks! 8 Sure Fire Ways to Take Advantage

Chapter 1 The Profile: Defining Characteristics & Strengths of an Entrepreneur

"Knowing what you want is the first and, perhaps, the most important step toward the development of persistence. A strong motive forces you to surmount many difficulties."
Napoleon Hill

In our profile, the usual identifying features do not really stand out. The individual portrayed could be male or female, young or old. Most striking in this picture are not the contours, size or shape of the face, but rather the *character* and the *qualities* which are evident within the individual's expression.

An entrepreneur is a person of *vision*; someone who takes *action*, and who has palpable *drive, initiative, focus* and *persistence*. In broad strokes, I'd like you to imagine someone who consistently calls forth the *courage* to take risks; and who continuously has the conviction to move forward without excuse or exception, despite all odds and obstacles.

In our cover silhouette can you envision *determination* set in the jaw; and eyes that are fixed on something not just spatially in the distance, but into the future, as well? There is confidence in the posture; and I'd also like you to imagine a nimble quality that permeates the pose, and renders the person both forthright and agile.

Does this profile describe you? Can you see aspects of yourself in this description? Do you possess the qualities and the character portrayed in this brief, biographical sketch? If not now, would you like to be able to answer, "Yes" at some point? Can you see yourself having the aspiration to fit this description?

Obviously, we are not born with these attributes. We must desire, aspire and work to develop them. You will need to be able to see and define your strengths as they relate to the requirements of building and running a business. Among these qualities, gifts and skills you will want to communicate effectively; be able to establish rapport and trust with individuals whom you haven't previously met; build long-term relationships; be able to tell your story with passion and enthusiasm, present the benefits of your products; and effectively manage your time.

Take a moment and think about your entrepreneurial growth areas as well as your existing strengths. Does this list scare and excite you? Do you see areas where you will need to spend time learning and practicing? Are there areas where you are very comfortable? I hope so. The great news is that you can earn while you are learning! And while the above characteristics and strengths are important, there is one attribute that is paramount! With this one quality your shortcomings become exciting challenges.

Chapter 2 In Life, as in the Dictionary, Enthusiasm Comes Before Entrepreneur

"The starting point of all achievement is desire."
Napoleon Hill

In life, as in the dictionary, the word "enthusiasm" comes before the word "entrepreneur." The word enthusiasm, from the Greek words *enthous* meaning "inspired" and *theos* meaning "god" refers to someone who is divinely inspired. Or, to put it another way, Webster's dictionary defines enthusiasm as: "passionate interest in or eagerness to do something; something that arouses a consuming interest."

Having a consuming interest in something about which you are excited and passionate, is positively delicious. Can you think of a time when you were so taken with something that it fascinated and delighted you? Something that you constantly thought and dreamed about, made plans to accomplish or took decisive action to fulfill? This is a rather typical feeling experienced by successful entrepreneurs.

According to the Oxford English Dictionary, entrepreneur is defined as, "a person who sets up a business or businesses, taking on greater

than normal financial risks in order to do so."
The word comes from the French, *entreprendre*
or enterprise, meaning "one who undertakes." I
like the creative and adventurous aspect of this.

A person who has a job works; an entrepreneur
creates. When serving others, or doing what we
love, it naturally feels more like joy than work.
Has your passion ever been ignited by such an
experience?

Many individuals remain in jobs they don't like
because they are unwilling to take risks. Yet it
can be far riskier to rely on others to determine
your future. Fear is a dominant emotion in many
people, and it has extinguished the aspirations
of countless individuals.

Napoleon Hill observed that there are positive
and negative emotions. The most powerful,
negative emotions are: fear, jealousy, hatred,
revenge, greed, superstition, and anger. Of the
positive emotions, the most powerful are: desire,
faith, love, sex, enthusiasm, romance and hope.
Hill wrote, "Positive and negative emotions
cannot occupy the mind at the same time. One
or the other must dominate." Every successful
entrepreneur understands this at some level,
and has developed the capacity to cultivate and
maintain their enthusiasm while undertaking
risks. It is a particular strength.

Understanding the importance of this ability,
and having the discipline to consistently do it, is

one of the distinguishing characteristics of almost everyone who is successful. And it seems absolutely necessary that, in life as in the dictionary, enthusiasm must come before one possesses the drive, determination and courage to become an entrepreneur.

Entrepreneurs are creators of business enterprises in which they want to achieve success, and frequently offer creative solutions with a heart for service. As Hill notes, "The starting point of all achievement is desire." You must possess a focused and sustained enthusiasm, which can actually take on a life of its own, in propelling you forward toward your desired results. This is a very energizing and enlivening experience.

There is a wonderful expression, "To Paddle Your Own Canoe." It is thought that the sentiment behind this expression might have originated with the words by Sextus Propertius (54 B.C.- A.D. 2) who said, "Let each man have the wit to go his own way." Someone who is independent and values self-reliance could be referred to as paddling their own canoe. Certainly, entrepreneurs embrace the understanding that we succeed only by being committed to our own vision and version of things. We also know that we must persist when others tend to quit.

This is where the quality and experience of enthusiasm comes in, in order to keep alive your vision, fuel your desire, and sustain your efforts.

Is it time for you to paddle your own canoe, and leave behind work, so that you are free to create the life you envision?

There are all kinds of entrepreneurs. For our purposes we are only going to look at home business opportunities. Specifically, Network Marketing, also referred to as multi-level marketing, and more broadly, as direct sales. Internet marketing is frequently a key approach in network marketing and other home-based businesses. There are several reasons why this book will focus on network marketing. The primary one is the tremendous cost of owning and operating a traditional brick and mortar business, which is beyond the reach of many people who are entrepreneurial. This may include renting or leasing property, inventory, insurance, payroll, healthcare, equipment, franchise fees and more. Network marketing is an ideal choice given the low start-up costs, and the fact that many companies have made the multi-million dollar up-front investment and offer systems you can plug into and begin earning commissions right away.

In addition to this, brick and mortar businesses depend on the health of the local economy. It used to be that the positions we could hold or the jobs we could get were limited to where we live, our educational and skill levels, and the number of others competing for the same spot. Thankfully, that simply isn't the case anymore. Now you can have an international business, live anywhere you chose, and with a smart phone and wireless internet connection you can be successful in internet marketing. With the current economy, record numbers of unemployed or underemployed individuals are finding a great opportunity in Network marketing.

There are also many kinds of home businesses. You can do just about anything from home today, including manufacturing small crafts, writing, doing affiliate marketing, and much more. Many traditional jobs now allow people to telecommute; and independent contracting positions are available for myriad tasks that are done via the Internet. These all have their pluses and minuses. For example when manufacturing small crafts, you must have capital to invest, skills to create, marketing savvy. You must get out and make contacts with retailers or attend craft fairs to sell your products. You will probably want to build a website with a shopping cart. Affiliate marketing networks make it easy to market any number of products via the Internet if you have capital to advertise and skills to do keyword research. A lot of the information and tips provided in this book can be applied to these home businesses, as well as helping you to enhance your personal relationships in general. This is because so many of the lessons you learn in a network marketing home business enable you to grow and develop as a person. The best home businesses are actually personal growth opportunities with a lucrative compensation plan included!

Thankfully, there are proven systems that make it possible for you to achieve your goals and live your dreams, without the enormous risks and huge capital outlay of the traditional brick and mortar business model. Obviously, it is important to find the one that is right for you. Like many, if not most network marketers, I tried several different opportunities before finding the company that is right for me.

This is the book I wish I had read before I started on this adventure, but couldn't find. That is why I wrote it. I have spent a significant amount of my professional career mentoring, coaching and nurturing growth in individuals just like you. It is an honor to be in a position to encourage others, and witness their increased insights, personal growth and realized success. I don't have to tell you that it is both a joy and a privilege to be a part of something that rewarding.

So, is a home business right for you? Let's take a closer look at some specific challenges and benefits.

Chapter 3 Is A Home Business Right for Me? 5 Key Challenges to Consider

"The value of decisions depends upon the courage required to make them."
Napoleon Hill

Given the reality of our faltering economy, more and more people are losing their jobs. In addition to this, a lot of people live with the stress that their job may be at risk at some point in the future. They live with an underlying anxiety that they can't shake off, predict or avoid that looming possibility.

Among those who are employed, many are actually underemployed. They are no longer in positions that recognize, utilize and reward the experience, skills and educational levels they have achieved. People with advanced college degrees are in minimum wage jobs, often more than one, just to cover their monthly bills.

In these uncertain times, more people than ever are seriously considering starting their own business; and we are seeing people attracted to home businesses in record numbers. And it is widely believed that these numbers are only going to continue to increase, because more and more individuals are researching the profession

14

and discovering that network marketing is now a proven, respected business model.

Deciding that you want to own your own home business is a very big decision; and one that most people simply cannot afford to take lightly. Especially since most new businesses fail within their first five years. There seem to be as many obstacles as there are rewards, and it takes a tremendous amount of commitment if you are actually going to succeed in your own business.

When trying to determine whether or not a particular home business opportunity is right for you, I believe there are several essential elements you must consider.

Ask yourself these questions:
- Does the opportunity excite, challenge and energize me?

- Does the company's mission fit with my vision and values?

- Are the products or services ones I believe in; and about which I am or could be passionate? Will I be able, with integrity, to enthusiastically share them with others?

- Do I personally use the products or am I willing to use them? Do the products offer real, significant benefits?

- Does the company have a proven track record?

- Does the company offer generous compensation?

- Is there a limit on how much I will be able to earn?

- Does the business opportunity provide a virtual back office and have powerful systems in place that I can plug into and follow at my own pace?

- Does the company include training, support and a community of other like-minded entrepreneurs with whom I can mastermind, grow and network?

- Am I truly willing to invest in myself, and do the work necessary to become successful?
- Will I be committed to learning, growing and being challenged?

- Will I follow the system of my chosen company and be coachable?

Below are some challenging realities which you will want to consider:

Some start-up costs are required.
As with any viable business, you will have to make an upfront investment; and typically, there are certain on-going monthly costs. These are often for consumable products for yourself; and there can be charges for tools, training and virtual back office support. These costs vary considerably from opportunity to opportunity, but none come close to the substantial investment of a traditional business. You will want to find out exactly what they are, and what they do and do not include. If you are not willing to make the necessary investment, then you are probably looking for a job or some form of employment, rather than for an actual business opportunity.

There are tangible risks involved
A home business is a real business and you will need to treat it as such: there are various compliance, tax, and possibly licensing issues to be considered. You must do your due diligence. Ask the person with whom you are exploring your business opportunity.

The responsibility rests with you.
Remember, you will be a business owner, not an employee. You can choose an opportunity which includes mentoring and/or coaching (and I strongly recommend you find an established leader

whom you respect); but it is up to you to work for and achieve the success you envision. You must be disciplined, motivated and a self-starter. As an employee, you generally have someone else, namely a boss, giving direction, imposing deadlines, setting goals. Now, staying motivated and doing the work will be up to you. Your failure or success is yours to determine. This is very freeing, but your work style and what motivates you will be an important consideration.

Like any successful business, you must continually build your customer base and team. There will be a certain amount of attrition; some members will not perform as well as you hope. Even though there is the promise and the reality of residual income, not everyone who comes into your business has the drive and commitment that you do. So you will want to keep growing your team and nurturing your team builders on an ongoing basis.

There is greater exposure and need for asset protection.
Unfortunately there are those who target businesses for frivolous lawsuits. So, at some point as you grow your business you will want to consider appropriate measures to protect yourself, your business and your assets.

It can be isolating without a community.

In an office setting, there can be unwanted politics, unfair treatment, favoritism and discrimination. But there can also be great teamwork, supportive colleagues and an atmosphere that encourages success. When you are working at home you will want to build the support systems you need in order to thrive. There are times when life will interrupt you. Often when I am talking with someone on the phone, my dogs will begin barking because out the front windows they suddenly see a coyote or two strolling by. It used to feel unprofessional to me, but now makes me smile because I am working at home doing what I love in a gorgeous setting.

It is extremely important to do your due diligence when evaluating the various opportunities available to you. Unfortunately, I have heard several stories from bright, conscientious individuals who got involved with something that either wasn't legitimate, or didn't offer any real training or support. There are people who have tried this business model and decided it wasn't for them for a variety of reasons. Many people quit because they are unrealistic about what is required and what they are willing to do. Others move from one opportunity to the next, thinking the grass is greener elsewhere and they never give themselves or their business the benefit of persistence and the time to succeed. This is why it is so important to answer the above questions to the best of your ability; and have a very candid conversation with those representing the opportunity or opportunities you are seriously considering.

For most of us who entered into the home business arena as a "newbie," with little or no prior experience, having a personal mentor and becoming part of a supportive team with a proven track record, was a very important component of our success.
I tried several opportunities and invested a great deal of money before finding the company, culture, mission and product line which is a truly inspiring and profitable fit for me.

Naturally, you can benefit from a variety of exceptionally good, leading edge products available only through companies within our industry. But without a solid company imbued with integrity; strong support from your upline leadership; simple, proven systems that can be readily duplicated; a generous compensation plan; and comprehensive training, it is very difficult to become and to remain successful over the long term as a business owner. I left my last company and joined my present company because, although I loved the products, they did not have the infrastructure, training and systems that allowed others to succeed as I did.

There are other, more personal, considerations you'll no doubt want to think about when trying to determine whether or not some type of home business opportunity is right for you. Is this the right time? Can you afford to do it? Can you afford not to? Hopefully, the above list will be helpful to you in your process, and serve to raise other important questions for you to consider.

Owning a home business is not for everyone. Yet, for many it is truly ideal. I have had people refer to having their own home business in these ways:

> "Finding this opportunity was an answer to prayer for my family and me."

> "This is the one thing in my life I've done right."
> "Even though it was scary and took longer than I thought it would to start making money, it's the best decision I've ever made."

> "I had no idea of the power of residual income before this. It's amazing."

Can you imagine being in a position to have someone, often in tears, say something like this to you? To be the one to whom they express their deep gratitude for your help in introducing them to your opportunity?

Now that we have explored some of the challenges, let's take a look at some of the benefits.

Chapter 4 Is A Home Business Right for Me? 5 Key Benefits

"There is a difference between wishing *for a thing and being* ready *to receive it. No one is ready for a thing until he believes he can acquire it. The state of mind must be* belief, *not mere hope or wish. Open-mindedness is essential for belief. Closed minds do not inspire faith, courage, or belief."* Napoleon Hill

Is a home business right for you? Only you can make that determination for yourself and your family. However I really encourage you to consider the possibility. Who knows, it could be the best decision you'll ever make. Consider some of the key benefits:

You have no commute or office politics
You can have a 10 second trip down the hallway, from your bedroom to your office; be free from the unprofessional gossip and posturing that can occur with co-workers; and not have the stress of a demanding and possibly unreasonable boss looking over your shoulder.

Time & money freedom; autonomy and independence

You can determine your own schedule, work when it is optimal for you and earn as much as you are willing to, based on your commitment and your own efforts. You are your own boss, and are in a position to define what motivates you to succeed, and why.

Break away from being a wage-earner and get into profits

There are many genuine, legitimate incentives for having your own business. In a wage-based system what you earn is limited to your hourly wage or salary and bonuses, and typically represents only one source of income. Your efforts go into making money for others and you are trading your time for money; so when you are not putting in the time, you no longer make any income. In a profit-based system, you have the opportunity to build multiple streams of income and are limited only by your imagination, efforts and results. Certain economic experts tell us that successful people have at least 3 sources of income - 2 of which are passive or residual. Residual income means that you are receiving current income based on work you have done previously, or from systems you have set up in the past. This is how individuals create true time, money and geographic freedom. You also gain tax advantages by being an owner vs. an employee. A conversation with your tax person will give you a good idea of all of the tax advantages to owning your own home business.

Your success is limited only by you
The only thing standing between you and success is finding the right opportunity, your level of enthusiasm, and your willingness to do what it takes.

Learning and applying new skills and increasing your value to others
It has been said that having your own home business is a wonderful personal growth opportunity with a compensation plan attached. I wholeheartedly agree! Learning about yourself, igniting your passion and providing high quality service to others while intentionally living your life by design rather than default, is incredibly rewarding.

If you think you can't do a home business, consider this anonymous quote:

> **"It's impossible," said Pride.**
> **"It's risky," said Experience.**
> **"It's pointless," said Reason**
> **"Give it a try," whispered the Heart.**

But why, oh why, might you want to follow your heart and embark on such an opportunity? This question is absolutely crucial in your decision-making process.

Chapter 5 The Power of Why

> *"Definiteness of purpose is the point from which one must begin...for it takes on animation, life and power when backed by a burning desire to translate that purpose into its material equivalent." Napoleon Hill*

Your Why is what drives you to succeed. It contains your vision of a better life, and better relationships. Living out your Why is happiness. Your Why is your purpose and your passion. It is the wellspring of your enthusiasm. It keeps you going despite challenges. It is the reason you don't quit. In looking at the meaning of vocation, Frederick Buechner writes, "Neither the hair shirt nor the soft berth will do. The place God calls you to is the place where your deep gladness and the world's deep hunger meet."

It is extremely important that you understand and define your Why. You need to be very clear about your purpose and the reason or reasons you are pursuing this kind of opportunity, and all that it entails. Always, always be true to yourself, as well as to your highest aspirations and deepest values. Here are some more questions to consider:

- Are you, or do you want to be, a leader with the character and qualities described in our illustrative profile of an entrepreneur?

- Are you seeking time freedom and the ability to enjoy more leisure with your family?

- Are you trading too much quality time for a job that demands more and more from you as lay-offs and downsizing continue to threaten the security of countless employees and your peace of mind?

- Is it money? Are you looking for complete freedom from debt, and a better lifestyle, or perhaps a more secure retirement?

- Would you like to be able to start a family foundation in order to have the capacity to donate to causes or issues you care about?

- Do you want to be able to completely fund your children's or grandchildren's college education?

- Do you have family members with significant health challenges, involving costly treatments toward which you would like to contribute?

- Are you a baby boomer, who lost part of your retirement savings in the stock market plunge and you want to replace your nest egg, as I have?

- Could it be that you long for geographic freedom; freedom that will enable you to travel whenever you want, and live wherever you choose?

When your Why is big enough, strong enough, and compelling enough, the "How" tends to take care of itself.

It is important to identify, define and envision the specific goals you want to achieve; develop a plan of action that you will undertake to reach your stated results; and ensure that your thoughts and beliefs are aligned in a way that will support your actions and the attainment of your goals. Without a roadmap it is too easy to wander aimlessly or get stuck. If you are looking for a get rich quick option, this is not for you.

Once you clearly define and embrace your Why, you will be pulled by your vision and propelled by your enthusiasm. Realize that you are enough, and trust that you will have what you need as things unfold. Remember your Why. And be gentle and patient with yourself, especially in the beginning.

So much will be coming at you, seemingly all at once. It is like there is this great dizzying array of divergent data and concept strands swirling all around you, seemingly at odds with each other - and it is hard to see how everything could possibly be woven together and form a real home business. Yet it does come together. And the sense of accomplishment you feel, the sheer exhilaration you experience at learning new skills, applying them, and then teaching them to others for their benefit, is positively delicious.

The home business model and Internet marketing explosion are changing the face of commerce and consumerism. It is extremely powerful because it offers an endless number of possibilities for the average person with above average dreams and drive.

There are many aspects to mastering network marketing, and each of us comes to this opportunity with varying degrees of experience and expertise. This is one reason your Why is so important. Think of the importance of your Why this way:

- When your Why isn't big enough, it's too easy to succumb to overwhelm, lose heart and become discouraged.

- Your Why is what motivates you, and your business coach or mentor helps guide you.

- Your Why is that radiant, compelling reason that enables you to keep striving in the face of one obstacle after the next. It will fuel your self-mastery, discipline and on-going hunger and excitement about learning.

- When you feel like quitting (and you will), remember Why you started in the first place.

- Without an irresistible Why, it is difficult to press on when the going gets tough. And it will get tough.

It is important to never let self-doubt or naysayers deter you or dampen your dreams. Don't dwell on what didn't work or on your mistakes – learn from them, incorporate your learning and move on. When we learn from our mistakes, they are transformed into lessons and have real value for us. I like to think of all the investments I've made that didn't give me the return I was hoping for, as tuition I have paid for important lessons. Viewed this way, they are not expensive losses, they are priceless learnings. It's up to you to decide how you view them; and whether or not you choose to utilize them for your benefit.

Like riding a horse, it is important to get back on when you've been thrown off. Maintain or regain your momentum; focus on your motivation and keep your passion ever before you. This is your dream, your vision, and your new reality. Don't lose sight of that no matter what obstructions appear in your path. Henry Ford said, "Obstacles are those frightful things you see when you take your eyes off your goal."

Remember always that you are a masterpiece in the making; and surely you and your Why are worth all of the focused, disciplined effort needed to become the fruitful and fulfilled person you were created to be. Understand that it is ultimately up to you to make it. While the weight of responsibility in that statement can feel daunting, the freedom it holds is even more powerful. Furthermore, if you position yourself on a great team, you will experience the exhilaration of being in business for yourself, but not by yourself. That is one of the most beautiful things about joining a winning team with deep integrity, whose members share your values.

So how do you stay focused, maintain your enthusiasm and honor your Why when life becomes a four-letter word, the stuff hits the fan, the wheels fall off your wagon, you're not having any fun and you just know it's going to be a bad hair day? Well, what if I told you there is a way you can avoid having any more bad hair days?

Chapter 6 No More Bad Hair Days in the Salon of Positive Thinking

"Positive and negative emotions cannot occupy the mind at the same time. One or the other must dominate. It is your responsibility to make sure that positive emotions constitute the dominating influence of your mind."   *Napoleon Hill*

It is deeply gratifying in today's faltering economy to be part of a profession that has proven accessible models for success. By providing the systems, tools and training necessary, the average person (with above average commitment) has the ability to take control of their future.

You do this by learning the system of your chosen opportunity; becoming a product of your products; experiencing and embracing the exciting paradigm shift in your thinking; and then developing the mindset and mastering the mechanics in order to enjoy financial and lifestyle freedom, all at your own pace.

Instinctively, you can see the wisdom in the adage, "Winners never quit and quitters never win." If you embrace this understanding, you too will be able to achieve your goals. There is a well-known Henry Ford quote that is both poignant and insightful. It is literally true, and for those who employ its power, there are virtually no limits to what can be achieved. It has everything to do with the way we look at things, and we can spend a lifetime penetrating its depths and applying it in our daily lives.

Henry Ford rightly observed, "Whether you think you can or think you can't - you are right." It seems impossible and counter-intuitive, that two statements -where each makes a claim that is the exact opposite of the other – can both be true. But such is the power of our thoughts.

Much more than some notion of wishful thinking, the power of visualization is an immutable force at work in the universe. Like gravity, this Law is at work at all times whether or not you believe it. You can say you don't believe in gravity, but the constancy of its pull and power continues to be exerted nonetheless. Everything within our universe is comprised of energy. Energy is flowing to, within and through you. With focused concentration, i.e. thinking, you can influence this flow. The more your thoughts are in alignment with your Why and your deep gladness, the more potent, harmonious and directed your energy will be.

Obviously, it makes sense to consider how you can apply this knowledge to your own life in order to assist you in achieving your goals and begin enjoying whole new dimensions of success. Why would anyone choose *not* to take advantage of something so accessible and transformative? You can either choose to employ this insight, or miss out on what it can do for you. It is remarkable how it works, and I love seeing others incorporating it, in order to enhance and transform their lives as well.

Naturally, many people recognize that our thoughts influence how we feel; and how we feel influences our actions. Our actions then lead to our results. This is a basic tenant of the Law of Attraction. I learned much of this from personally studying with Bob Proctor.

There are times we all allow ourselves to get irritated. Maybe we begin thinking it is going to be a "bad hair day." Or we say we got up "on the wrong side of the bed." Sometimes we feel frustrated and impatient with ourselves or someone else, and we dwell on those thoughts and feelings until they begin to significantly impact our day.

As soon as I become aware of these thoughts or feelings, I make a conscious effort to shift my thinking and re-align my energy. I also recite Psalm 51:10, "Create in me a clean heart, O God; and renew a right spirit within me." Your language may be different, but the process is the same. For me, this works every time – usually immediately. At first it takes a conscious, concerted effort. Over time and with discipline and practice it naturally becomes easier.

If I am really feeling put out (or don't recognize right away what I'm doing), I may have to focus my thoughts for a longer period of time. Eventually, it always works.
Of course, there are times when I am momentarily attached to being whiny and miserable and self-righteous and indignant. On the rare occasions when that happens – once my self-awareness kicks in - I have a good laugh at myself, and my poopy mood disappears like a mist in brightening sunlight.

One of my favorite stories comes from the Cherokee wisdom tradition. It is called the Story of Two Wolves. It touched me so deeply that I paired two of my photographs with it and created a poster and a greeting card. I share this story in the next chapter.

Chapter 7 The Story of Two Wolves

One evening an old Cherokee told his grandson about a battle that goes on inside people.

He said, "My son, the battle is between two "wolves" inside us all. One is Evil. It is anger, envy, jealousy, sorrow, regret, greed, arrogance, self-pity, guilt,
resentment, inferiority, lies, false pride, superiority, and ego. The other is Good. It is joy, peace, love, hope, serenity, humility,

kindness, benevolence, empathy, generosity, truth, compassion, and faith."

The grandson thought about it for a minute and then asked his grandfather, "Which wolf wins?" The old Cherokee simply replied, "The one you feed."

The point of this ancient story is that we must take full responsibility for ourselves and our thoughts, emotions, actions and results. We can recognize this and appreciate the resonant, empowering joy that accompanies it; or we will be living with varying degrees of discontent and disappointment. We each need to realize that we, and we alone, decide which "wolf" to feed. If we are still caught in the deceptive and seductive folly of blaming others for our situation, it is much more difficult to fully engage and harness this distinctive power.

When we are busy rationalizing, making excuses, blaming and diverting attention away from ourselves, we dilute our ability to draw on our beliefs. I like the analogy that if I am looking to someone else as the cause of my plight, and I am metaphorically pointing my finger at them in accusation or blame, I must notice that three of my fingers are pointing back at me. When I look away from the other, and focus on myself instead, I can usually uncover my part in whatever is occurring. Only then can I re-direct my thoughts and re-align my energy.

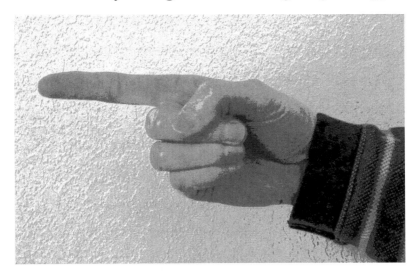

If you regularly apply this with discipline, you will never have another "bad hair day." Bad moments? Yes. Bad days? No.

The focused energy of your belief is always in play, and you absolutely can employ it for your own joy and success. "Whether you think you can or think you can't - you are right." Therefore, think you can, know you can, believe with energy, enthusiasm and a deep sense of expectation and gratitude that you have already attained it; and you will.

Remember "The Little Engine That Could" with its constant refrain, "I think I can, I think I can, I think I can," and so it did?

Seeing that it is possible for others is the first step. Or to put it another way, I can tell you that it works for me and many, many others; so it can work for you. You need to extend this to include yourself in the knowing, so that you now see and lay claim to the realization that it is also possible for you.

Believe it, do it, keep on doing it. As you do, it becomes easier and easier. You'll also be able to recognize when those "bad hair day" thoughts start, and you can head them off at the pass. It's up to you, it's in your power, and you absolutely can re-align your energy and become the powerful force who does. Let's look at some other resources that can help you understand, embrace and incorporate this potent realization.

Chapter 8 Purpose, Balance, Success & Leadership

"Extinguish your fears.
Listen to your heart. Ignite
your passion."
Linda Compton

It is important to realize that if you are wholeheartedly engaged in your business, it becomes an extension of you, and an expression of your integrity. I often say that my home business isn't just what I do, it is who I am. My business enterprise is wonderfully all-encompassing and feels like my calling.

It's up to you to do the work necessary to succeed, and often this means changing your priorities and making hard choices. You are responsible for setting your goals and striving for your success. The people with whom you spend the most time have a significant influence on you. You want to be committed to learning and growing and, if necessary, hugging the naysayers in your life good-bye.

You need to be (or work to become) a self-starter and an action-taker who is decisive. You want to truly and deeply believe that you can and therefore will, succeed: to be of one heart and mind, not divided or undecided, but knowing your destiny is yours to design.

Happiness, gratitude and the capacity to forgive are choices we make. We choose to be unhappy or happy; to be ungrateful or grateful; to be unforgiving or forgiving. And finally, you must be persistent and absolutely resolute about finding a way when none appears to exist.

Living into these concepts brings a special clarity and boldness which can help with honing your purpose, achieving balance in your life and work, while leading to success in the place where your deep gladness and the world's current needs meet. It also tends to foster leadership skills.

Symbols can be a powerful way to represent and convey meaning. The Zia Sun is a wonderful example which symbolizes the fullness of life, imbued with purpose, balance and values. It is the symbol on the State flag of New Mexico, and a fitting representation of our state's long, rich and diverse history.

The Zia Pueblo Indians regard the sun as sacred. Their symbol for the sun is a red circle, open in the center, with four groups of four rays each, emanating from the center in each of the four directions. For the Zia Indians, four is a sacred number and represents life, nature, character and spirit. There are also the four seasons: spring, summer, autumn and winter. There are the four directions: North, South, East and West. They recognize the four periods of each day: morning, afternoon, evening and nighttime. And there are the four seasons of life: childhood, youth, middle age and old age.

Zia Indians have a deep belief that life comes with four sacred obligations which must be developed throughout one's lifetime: a strong body, clarity of mind, a pure spirit, and a genuine commitment to the welfare of others. Achieving these qualities represents a successful life. This so eloquently captures the importance of balance, health, wholeness, wisdom, generosity and a heart for service.

The lesson and the practice is this: To grow and advance with value - meaning to give value first (before asking for anything). To realize that receiving always follows giving. And to understand that we must always make a meaningful contribution before we can expect any real compensation. These are among the lessons that further the making of a leader. It is very clear that in order to be successful, it is absolutely imperative that we first increase our own value to others.

This is the reason so much emphasis is placed on mindset. In today's world we hear more about competition than cooperation; more about greed than generosity. It seems that as our broken economy worsens and people's fears are heightened, a kind of "me first" survivalist mentality threatens to overshadow our greater selves.

It is important to resist this understandable tendency as we strive to develop the characteristics and qualities of a successful life, including leadership through service. I believe the most potent way to achieve this is to extinguish your fears, listen to your heart and ignite your passion. We will look at some of the ways to achieve this in the next chapter.

Chapter 9 Wages, Profit, Ownership & Adventure

"One day, something clicks. All those inspirational and motivational quotes, a lifetime of experiences and learning align. A stunning flash of insight floods your heart. There is no going back, no unknowing. No more pretending, hiding, seeking, making apologies for being or any excuses for doing. Every breath is recognized as a gift, each thought and action understood as a personal responsibility. Every moment seen and embraced as sacred and delicious. "
Linda Compton

To begin living an even fuller, more abundant, contribution rich life, you may need to let go of some former ways of thinking and doing; and cultivate some new ones. This is another reason so much emphasis is placed on mindset.

Perhaps your biggest challenge, if you have worked for someone else most of your life, will be changing your self-understanding. This comes as you begin seeing yourself not as an employee, but as a business owner.

Or maybe you have worked for yourself for many years, but need to learn to be receptive to a different business model; and become flexible and coachable once again. This isn't your traditional mom and pop shop. Many brick and mortar businesses are failing, and Corporate America as we've known it, rarely exists. Job security is scarce, and now most people have a series of careers or different work experiences throughout the course of their lives.

There have been some profound changes which are still hard for many to fully grasp. We have swiftly moved from the Industrial Age to the Information Age. If you are going to be in business for yourself, you need to understand how significant it is to transition from being a paid employee to being a business owner. While the challenges within a profit system are many and great, the freedom and autonomy, tax advantages, and numerous rewards are amazingly enriching.

As with any business, your success depends on your vision, motivation, influence, passion, persistence, and willingness to work hard. Working for someone else is an obligation; being in business for yourself is an adventure.

Why network marketing is the adventure worth sharing

When we are excited about something, perhaps it's a new movie, a restaurant, or some new product we've discovered, we are likely to tell our friends about it. We are sharing our joy and wanting them to have an opportunity to experience what we have found to be of value.

Network marketing is based on our referrals of a product or service that we believe in, to those we care about or others who are in our sphere of influence. You are networking, referring and enthusiastically sharing with others all the time.

The difference is, in network marketing you get paid every time someone acts upon your recommendation if you have a qualified affiliation with that company. How many times have you recommended a wonderful restaurant, a new movie, bottle of wine, health and beauty item, vacation spot, etc.? Did you receive a commission for thoughtfully sharing your positive experience?

With networker marketing companies, they have chosen a different distribution model. They do not have the traditional overhead costs of advertising. Instead, they put much of that money into the commissions paid to distributors and into product development. The products are often based on cutting edge science and are frequently better than products produced and sold conventionally. Direct sales products and services focus on providing innovative solutions to common problems and everyday needs.

Because they depend on referrals to make sales, network marketing companies are based on team support and cooperation versus competition. Sales are based on building long-term relationships and focus on serving others. In a brick and mortar business, you sell your products to whomever walks in the door. In network marketing, you have a greater ability to choose those with whom you'd like to work.

Technology has also dramatically changed the way we do business. We are no longer limited to only those people we know. With social media, affiliate marketing and the Internet, we have access to large groups of people that we have never met.

Given all of this, how do you go about finding the right opportunity? Is there some kind of criteria? If you feel excited about this business model, how do you decide which opportunities are viable and which ones should be avoided and why? In the next chapter you will hear from Billi Grossman, RDN who is a business partner and trusted friend. Her experience in network marketing makes her contribution of this chapter a valued addition. She offers five key considerations for choosing the opportunity that is right for you.

Chapter 10 5 Key Considerations for Choosing the Right Opportunity
Contributed by Billi Grossman, RDN

> *"Successful leaders must understand and apply the principle of cooperative effort and be able to induce followers to do the same. Leadership calls for power, and power calls for cooperation." Napoleon Hill*

Choosing the right company does not guarantee that you will be successful, but it does increase the likelihood and you will have more fun and adventure along the way. There are numerous considerations. Here we offer a starting point with questions relating to five considerations of primary importance.

Products
Many people come for the products first and build a business secondarily. So a good and saleable product is critical.

- Are the products unique? You want to be able to explain them in terms of benefits. What sets your products apart from any competition?

- Are they consumable? It is 5 to 10 times easier to keep a customer than to get a new one. You want a product that people will use and buy over and over again.

- Is there a need? Would people want to buy them whether they make money or not? Yours might be the greatest product in the world, but if it is not something that people want and need, you won't sell many.

- Do you like and believe in the products? Do you or would you use them? In order to represent the product well, you must know it. The best way to gain an understanding is to be a "product of the product." Using the product builds your belief in the benefits and helps you create a passionate, emotional story to share with others. Belief in your product makes your story all the more compelling.

- Do they work? The product must have a track record of doing what it claims to do. If there are scientific statements, are they based on real science and solid research? It is unlawful for companies to claim that their products cure any health issue, as they can be shut down by the Federal Trade Commission.

- Are they evergreen? Will they be around for years to come or are they based on the latest fad? Products that are timeless can help you build residual income for a lifetime.

- Who will use this product? You want a company that has enough selections to meet the needs of a wide range of individuals and lifestyles. A wider variety and selection means that your products will serve a large number of customers.

The Compensation or Marketing Plan
Your potential company will provide you with information about how its compensation plan is structured. Look at this information carefully and review it several times until you understand it. In addition to volume compensation, most companies provide introductory or new member bonuses, rank advancement bonuses and leadership bonuses. These may be paid daily, weekly, monthly, quarterly or yearly, though most companies pay monthly. Many companies increase the percentage of volume compensation as you advance up the ranks.

There are several questions you should ask when reviewing a company's compensation plan. Your income is based both on product sales and the sales of others that you recruit into your organization.

- Are you able to make money in the beginning by sponsoring an initial 2-3 people?

- Can anyone make money regardless of whether they have experience in network marketing?

- Is it supportive of building a large organization?
- Does the compensation plan support cooperative team building?

- What are the qualifying factors to getting paid?

- Aside from compensation paid on business volume, what bonuses are paid?

- How and when are commissions paid?

- How frequently has the compensation plan changed over the life of the company?

- Has there ever been an issue with people getting paid?

- Does the plan pay on the wholesale price or the retail price?

- How much product do you, personally, have to purchase to remain active to qualify for commissions?

- What, if any, is the refund policy?

There are 4 basic compensation plan structures used by most, if not all, of the network marketing companies. These are:

Matrix - Sometimes called Forced Matrix, this is the most complicated type of plan within which to earn money. It is easy to explain as it looks like a box. The Matrix is designed to grow quickly. Matrix plans limit how many people you may personally recruit and how deep you can build, for example it might pay you 3 wide x 7 deep. Any people you recruit beyond your width limit spill over into subsequent levels. At the end of the month, any volume which is not paid, goes away.

This plan is not as rewarding for people who are high producers and it is very important that everyone in the box is sponsoring others. On average 80% of the people who join network marketing companies join as product users and never sponsor another person which makes compensation within this structure more difficult to achieve.

Unilevel - There is no team aspect to the Unilevel structure. This plan requires you to sponsor a lot of people on your first level. Typically, companies using Unilevel pay a percentage through limited depth. There are often several qualifying markers that must be met before commissions are paid. For example, there may be a minimum number of "legs" started before the compensation kicks in or you may have to have a certain volume on one or several legs before you get paid on any leg. Some Unilevel plans only count a certain percentage of the volume of your strongest leg toward your commission. Unilevel plans pay monthly and any excess volume is cancelled every month, meaning you start fresh and must meet your volume markers each and every month.

Stair Step Breakaway - This is the most popular structure among companies. Like the Unilevel, in this plan you have to build several legs and each new personal recruit begins a new leg. There is often a limit to how deep the plan will pay. This structure also only pays through a limited number of levels. Higher commissions are given based on achieving larger numbers of personal recruits, i.e. stairs. Stair Step Breakaway plans are great for leaders but are not as good for those who only have a few people on their team.

Stair Step Breakaway plans allow enrollees who produce more than their sponsor to "Break Away" from the sponsor's volume. You may still be paid on the person's volume as long as your rank exceeds theirs, but usually at a much lower rate. This is demotivating for sponsors to help their people build. It also results in some unhealthy practices such as front end loading, which is the sponsor purchasing a large amount of volume themselves in order to keep up and not lose the income from the builder who has surpassed them.

In the Stair Step Breakaway structure, unpaid volume goes away at the end of each month.

Binary - With the Binary plan you build only 2 legs and build depth. There are several variations to binary plans. One popular variation, the 2-up plan, requires you to give commissions from your first 2 sales to your enroller. Some companies only pay through a certain number of levels. Many companies require you to build evenly on both sides and pay you on your lowest volume, but this is rather difficult to accomplish. Look for a plan that pays through all levels, does not cancel out banked volume and calculates commissions on a 2/3 - 1/3 ratio.

While some compensation plans are easier to work and understand than others, all of the structures allow some individuals to make money. The key is choosing a company with the structure that will work for you.

Most companies allow you to come back in with a new business center once you achieve the maximum earning or recruits in your initial compensation center. This is called Re-entry. In some companies re-entry is required upon reaching a certain business volume. Where you come in is important. Most companies restart you underneath your original center. When you come in at the bottom, you may have several completely separate centers to manage and your percentage of compensation paid on volume may decrease.

When a company starts your new center above your initial organization, it is both easier to manage and increases your total compensation. In such a structure, your original organization becomes one side of your team. Then you continue to build by filling up the other side. Coming in at the top also increases motivation for team building and helping others succeed.

Marketing Tools and Training

- What does it take to enroll with the company? Most companies have an initial membership fee to set up your account, provide access to a back-office with a sales website and customer service. In order to maintain active status and receive commissions, rebates, or bonuses, the associate must then purchase a minimum amount of volume each month.

- Is there a web-based ordering and enrolling system that is personalized to you? You will likely get a website that is similar to the one your enroller showed you when they talked to you about their opportunity. You can evaluate the ease of navigation and clarity of information from what you have been shown.

- Does the Company have sales materials developed or do you have to create your own? Do they have a social media presence? Again, your enroller may have shown you several pieces of information. When you ask questions, they will provide you with a variety of informational materials and very likely will include you in a conference call with someone higher up in the organization.

- What kind of training and support is available for associates? Is it companywide or solely from your "team". What is the cost, if any, for the training modules? Does the company sponsor conferences? Are they reasonably accessible? There should be some companywide training at a cost that is low enough that most new people can participate. While you want and will likely receive some training from your immediate sponsor, this should not be the sole source. Not everyone is a good trainer or has the skills to effectively support and manage a team. You also don't want to be dependent on one person for training and support because people do sometimes change companies.

- Is there a simple system for building your business that is easy to explain? A simple system of prospecting, presenting and enrolling with an easily understood compensation plan leads to higher duplication. Duplication is the process of helping others to prospect, present and enroll. A simple, concise system means an easier time for you and your team members to obtain good results in advancing through the ranks and building the team.

Company Longevity and History
More than 1000 network marketing companies start every year. 90% of them fail within their first 2 years. Although in the early years of Network Marketing it was true that those who joined early made it big. Now, with the right compensation plan, the playing field is more level. Lots of people are making big money in established companies in a very short period of time.

Another clue is how and where the company is growing. Are they growing in your local market, say North America? Network Marketing companies grow in a fairly predictable manner.

At the start of the Company, products are formulated. The compensation plan is created. Corporate management is hired and usually includes some established leaders in the profession. This is a vulnerable time for a company because it costs money to create products and systems. During this stage, the product may be reformulated a number of times which is expensive and puts pressure on both the company and those trying to sell the product. In addition, the compensation plan may be altered to allow for more cash flow to the company.

Then, a customer base is established. Growth is generally slow and steady. The company usually continues to develop products during this phase.

Once the company has a strong customer base, growth speeds up. Fast growth tests the infrastructure and there may be some glitches to be worked out. Many companies do not survive because they cannot produce enough, provide poor customer service, or run out of capital.

As growth increases, a period called Momentum occurs. This is when most new distributors join. The company is growing exponentially. Many companies bring on new leadership and transform their infrastructure and compensation plans at this time. If a company is not prepared for this kind of growth, they may fail.

Then growth slows and sales become fairly consistent. The company now has brand recognition, which may be either positive or negative. Some companies pull resources from their established market in order to expand globally. Does the company you are considering have the infrastructure to support global expansion?

You may hear people talking about getting in on the ground floor of an opportunity, but for people who are new to network marketing, this is not advisable. Seasoned marketers with significant experience and a large following can have success with start-ups because they know the industry and have weighed the risks. Look for a company between 5 and 15 years old. You want to join an organization that has worked through the bugs of start-up and has proven products and systems but has not yet saturated their market.

Culture and Ownership
- Does the Company and its leadership have integrity?

- Do they have a vision that aligns with yours?

- Are the policies supportive of the associates?

- Are they attracting strong networking leaders?

- Does the culture of the company encourage commitment to downline success? Is the person recruiting you someone who will coach, motivate and train you?

- Is the company a member of the Better Business Bureau, Direct Selling Association or other professional organizations?

- What awards have they earned? Have they been featured in any industry publications?

- Is the management a mix of successful people from the Networking Profession? Do the leaders have experience in the field? Have they built previous companies that grew to high sales volume?

- Are the company well capitalized? Is there enough money to maintain a solid infrastructure, keep pace with technology and business growth?

So, what happens if and when you find a company that excites you and meets your criteria? Can you do it? You may think to yourself, "I am not the sales type." Although your income is based on moving products through your network, the success of your business is much more dependent upon sharing your story than actually selling.

Finally, remember that any business is going to take a commitment of time. Do your homework, make your decisions and investment and stick with it. Make a 3-5 year commitment for your business to pay you a full-time income. Many people build their business in the pockets of their time, while remaining in their day job: 15 minutes here and there; networking at their child's soccer game, for example.

One of the key benefits of this type of business is that you can earn as you learn. Know that you will have to put in the time and do the work, but you don't have to know everything before you start. Remember that people spend years learning a job or getting a professional degree. It will take some time to master the ins and outs, but you can begin to earn income in the first few months if you are willing to follow a system and the lead of your sponsor. This also means spending time on personal development and product knowledge, in addition to the business tasks.

Next you will learn more of Linda's story.

Chapter 11 Your Heart's Desire, Solutions & Passion for Service

"Becoming your personal best is not about besting somebody else. It's about being better today than you were yesterday"
Linda Compton

A defining moment

Her comment yesterday really got me thinking. It was a statement carrying an element of surprise, mingled with relief, appreciation and even a compliment. She had a few important questions, and was also serious about needing to "do something."

She said, "I appreciate how you listen, and that you answer my questions without trying to pressure or sell me." I am guilty of enthusiasm, yet I hope I am never perceived or experienced as pressuring.

She was telling me that she wants to lose weight and have more energy. I know we can help her with that. It's that simple. The burden on my heart is to clearly communicate the solutions we offer, in a way that helps others freely make informed decisions. That's really it.

Integrity, increase and doing the irresistible

Do I represent a company with integrity and quality products I use daily and deeply believe in? Yes. If I help an individual acquire some of these products will I be paid? Yes, generously so. Compensation is great, and the more money one has, the more one can do and share.

However, money is just one tool among many. I value all kinds of tools, resources, options, and the ability to make a difference. The income stream is important, while the feeling I get when I motivate, inspire, or help someone effectively work toward their goals, is beyond important to me. It is precious. Sound corny? So be it. Why? Because it's true, and I simply wouldn't trade this feeling for anything.

Working within your integrity, honoring your heart's desire and promoting expansive increase becomes simply irresistible.

Accountability, choices and contributions

Some people will not understand, and that used to bother me. Not any longer. I have lived more years than I am going to live, and that realization changes one's perspective. I believe that I will be held accountable for the contributions I withhold, as well as for the ones I make.

I believe that God or Source uses every experience we have ever had to inform and empower our current work. As long as we are still here, we are not finished. There is more life, more learning, more giving and receiving that is meant for us. No matter what we have accomplished to this point, we are called to use our gifts in some form of service to others.

There is nothing else I'd rather be doing, and I am living my dream. In some ways I am working harder than ever, but it is with joy, grace and ease, rather than with stress and draining external demands. This business model is not one with a power-over approach, but rather it is one of cooperation, mutual benefit and empowerment. Therefore, I am energized and excited. The difference is like night and day.

There are those who say, "Do what you love and the money will follow." I think the sentiment is true, but incomplete. There needs to be discipline and consistency and some other key elements.

Life lessons: some expensive, some priceless

After I finished my first Master's degree, my Mom wanted me to go on and get my Ph.D. I told her it was too expensive. She said that she would pay for it. I smiled and thought to myself, "That is what makes it too expensive." When we live our lives fulfilling the dreams and expectations of others, it can cost us dearly. Sometimes too dearly.

If we do anything with a feeling of resentment, we are doing it for the wrong reasons or with some kind of disingenuous motive. If we are conflicted or have a divided heart, it might be better to say, "No thank you." Resentment is a sign of a divided heart and it is always on us; it is our responsibility. We have resentment toward another when we allow them to influence us to somehow step outside our own integrity, comfort level or personal preferences. But no one can do that without our permission.

How much are you willing to give, and to give up? What is it that most matters to you? I have often said if you show me your checkbook register and your credit card statements, I can tell you exactly what you value, regardless of what you say your priorities are. We always seem to find the money and the time for what we truly want, and we also value what we pay for.

I'll share a personal example with you. When I moved to New Mexico, I paid for professional movers to transport my furnishings. Given my art collection, I had increased insurance. One of my paintings was badly damaged, and a representative came to the house to look at the torn and soiled box in which the painting had been professionally packed. After examining the broken glass and the torn canvas, as well as my documentation, he agreed that full replacement value was in order. Expecting me to be delighted, he was surprised by my response.

While grateful for the insurance, it simply couldn't replace the art.

He said he was authorized to write me a four-figure check. What he didn't understand was that I'd had that amount of money before. And I chose to spend it on the painting. I didn't want the money; I wanted the painting. It was an original and it was beyond repair. This experience highlighted one aspect of the very real inadequacies and limits of money.

Your heart's desire and your personal best

So, I think the key truly is to find your heart's desire and to pursue it wholeheartedly. Frequently it is beyond challenging to uncover your passion, since it can be buried beneath the expectations of others; it can get shoved to the bottom of your list; or dimmed by self-doubt.

A great antidote for these obstacles can frequently be found in doing different things for others, in order to see what makes your heart sing. Some kind of service; the kind that is not a chore or a burden, but rather one that brings you joy. This is freely giving of yourself to something higher and greater than we are.

A good way to determine this is to discern whether something enervates you or energizes you. Does it diminish or does it lead to increase; does it break down or does it build up? Our heart's desire usually springs from the startling awareness and appreciation of all that we have, and all that we are.

With this realization can come a burning desire to give back, by extending ourselves and giving forth. We do this by first extinguishing our fear, then listening to our heart and igniting our passion. As we become our personal best, we can offer the best of ourselves to a hurting world. Being an entrepreneur is one very special way to do that.

Entrepreneurs are often individuals with innovative solutions to society's most pressing problems. We are generally passionate and persistent, feel inspired to tackle some of the major social issues, coming up with new ideas for wide-scale change.

Rather than leaving societal needs to the government or conventional business sectors, many entrepreneurs identify problems and create solutions.

For example, the co-founders of the company with which I am affiliated came out of an extremely comfortable retirement because of the alarming rate of obesity, the level of toxicity in our environment, the heightened levels of disease, the state of our food supply and of our declining physical health. They have a vision and are on a mission to change world health, while freeing people from physical and financial pain.

After losing too many people I care about to disease, bearing witness to the crushing challenges of financial stress; being saddened by wide-spread, ill-informed lifestyle choices; and lack of optimal nutrition, I found solutions that changed my life and that are transforming the lives of lots of everyday people. This is the heady mix of problems and creative solutions, from which inspiration springs.

What deeply concerns you? About what are you most passionate? Do you have a fervent desire to be part of the solution? If you could be an effective change agent, would that make your heart sing? This is the kind of resolute enthusiasm which motivates many entrepreneurs.

If this sounds like you, let's look next at some key next steps.

Chapter 12 Get it in Gear, Baby!

"Do not wait. The time will never be 'just right.' Start where you stand, work with whatever tools you may have at your command, and better tools will be found as you go along." Napoleon Hill

Is a home business right for you? Have you looked at a few networking companies and identified one that reflects your values and passion? If so, now is the time to get started!

These steps are loosely in priority order and there is room for flexibility and discretion. This list is meant to be a general guide. What is important is that you cultivate a deep thirst for learning and acquiring new skill sets over time. One thing about the Internet is that it is constantly changing and evolving and we need to keep growing, as well. Don't get bogged down trying to learn everything before you begin (because you can't anyway). Resist thinking you need to know enough to feel comfortable before you get started. You don't. Don't spend too long getting ready. You will be able to learn and apply new skills as you go along. It will all come together; it will start making sense. And remember, in the midst of it all, it's supposed to be fun! For example, in my company it is essentially as simple as one, two, three. You become a product of our products, learn our plug and play system, and share your story.

After you have done your due diligence and decided upon the opportunity that is right for you, it's time to get it in gear.

- Define your work area. You will need a desk or table that is conducive to being productive, a computer with high speed Internet and a phone.

- Determine what your work schedule will be and commit to a specific amount of time that will be dedicated to building your business. Create a daily schedule which includes 3-5 income producing activities. This will keep you organized and on task.

- Realize that there is never a perfect time, so it is important to dive in. Sign up, make your initial investment and follow the recommended procedures for your chosen business.

- Familiarize yourself with the key features and benefits of your business opportunity. Get to know the leadership, the products or services, and the compensation plan. Begin to attend training and networking calls and events.

- Set up everything in such a way that you are in compliance with all local, state and federal laws (or the laws of your particular province or country). This is not optional! It is important to be professional, keep detailed records and treat your business like a business. It is not a hobby.

- Determine your business plan. Many networking companies have business plans and systems in place. If this is the case, follow the leader is your best course of action. Find someone who has achieved the goals you want to reach and do what they did to get there. If you find a proven system, follow it. Don't try to re-invent the wheel.

- Think of your goals. What do you need to accomplish this week? This month? Where do you see yourself in a year?

- Learn about all the different types of advertising (paid, low-cost, and free).

- Understand how social media (Twitter, Facebook, etc.) works, consider blogging; and establish your online brand.

Now is the time to get your wonderful new business in gear! Remember the wise counsel of Napoleon Hill.

"Do not wait.

The time will never be 'just right.'

Start where you stand,

work with whatever tools

you may have at your command,

and better tools will be found

as you go along."

Napoleon Hill

Glossary of Network Marketing Terms

Compiled by Billi Grossman, RDN

ABO - Associate Back Office (see *back office*)

Affiliate - A person or another company who is in association with a company. Companies often establish affiliate relationships through a network with sellers who advertise the product with a designated link to a *sales page* and are paid a commission for each sale generated through that link.

Associate - Someone who enrolls in a *network marketing* business and meets the company's qualifications. There is usually an enrollment fee to set up the account and the *associate* agrees to purchase a certain dollar amount or volume of products each month. Associates receive wholesale buying privileges and earn commissions.

Autoship - A selection of products that ships to the customer automatically in regular intervals, i.e. monthly. Autoships may be required to meet a minimum order size and remain eligible to earn commissions.

Back Office - A duplicated or replicated website within a company that provides product information, policies, enrollment and order portals. Can frequently be customized by the *associate*.

Brand - Your brand is what you are known for and the way you market yourself. It includes your integrity, reputation, and *niche*. It is reflected in all the ways you promote your business.

Business builder - Generally refers to someone who is in a Network Marketing company with the intention of recruiting others into the business and creating their own team.

Business Opportunity - The business system in which associates can earn income.

Business Volume (BV) - The numerical point system attached to the volume of sales for your networking organization. Business volume is usually slightly less than the actual dollar volume of sales.

Compensation plan - The way an *associate* or *business builder* gets paid based on *business volume* and recruiting in a network marketing company. Also called Marketing Plan.

Connecting - Meeting new people and *prospecting* them for your networking business.

Crossline - Someone who is sponsored by your *upline* leader but is not associated with your personal team.

Downline - People you recruit and train, and whose sales volume generates commissions for you.

Direct Sales - Sales made directly to an end-user; typically through a party plan, internet marketing, or one-on-one demonstrations.

Duplication - Teaching others to sell products and recruit members in order to build your organization.

Enroller - The person who recruits and enrolls another in a networking business. Also referred to as a sponsor.

Entrepreneur - The owner, manager or founder of a business enterprise.

Financial Freedom - Having sufficient wealth to do the things you enjoy and desire without debt.

Front end loading - Purchasing a large amount of volume themselves in order to keep up with commissions and not lose income from the builder who has surpassed them.

Home Business - A small business that operates primarily from the business owner's home office.

Independent Distributor - A business or person that distributes a product for the manufacturer. The distributor is responsible for the cost of operating their business, taxes, etc.

J-O-B - Slang for Just-Over-Broke

Members - Anyone who enrolls in a network marketing company. There is usually an enrollment fee to set up the account.

Multilevel Marketing (MLM) - A form of *direct sales* where *associates* are able to purchase products at wholesale; build a consumer network of others who may also offer, represent or distribute the products. Compensation is based on sales volume and recruiting. Associates advance through compensation and recognition ranks depending on their performance. Also called *Network marketing*.

Network Marketing - A form of *direct sales* where *associates* are able to purchase products at wholesale, build a consumer network of others who may also distribute the products. Compensation is based on sales volume and recruiting. *Associates* advance through compensation and recognition ranks depending on their performance. Also called Multilevel marketing.

Niche - A place or position suitable or appropriate for a person or thing. Often refers to a subset of a market on which a specific product is focused. The market niche defines the product features and aims at satisfying specific needs.

Opportunity meeting - A gathering of marketers and *prospective product users and/or individuals interested in the business,* at which the *business opportunity* is presented.

Passive Income - Income received on a regular basis that requires little effort to maintain. Also called *Residual Income.*

Personal Volume (PV) - The numerical point system attached to the volume of products that you personally purchase in a networking company. Personal volume is usually slightly less than the actual dollar volume of purchases.

Personally sponsored - People in your networking organization that you have personally *recruited* and enrolled.

Preferred customer (PC) - Someone who enrolls in a networking company, usually with *autoship*, who is allowed to purchase products at the wholesale price but is not eligible to receive commissions.

Presentation - Showing your customer the features and benefits of your products either by telling your *story* or using a *tool* (video, audio, printed).

Product user - An enrollee of a *network marketing* company who never *recruits* or *enrolls* others.

Prospect - A potential *team* member. Someone who is interested in or has a need for your products or business system

Prospecting - Approaching a potential *team* member and sharing your opportunity.

Rank Advancement - Moving up within a company's compensation structure based on personal performance. Rank advancements are designed to encourage increased sales and *recruiting*.

Re-entry - Starting a new business center after achieving the maximum earning or recruits in an initial compensation plan.

Recruit - A new enrollee, is a person you have personally *sponsored* but who has not enrolled anyone yet.

Recruiting - The actions taken once a prospect has indicated interest and before they have actually enrolled, for example, sending more information, following up, answering questions.

Residual Income - Recurring income received on a regular basis that requires little effort to maintain. Also called *Passive Income.*

Sales Page - A one page website that provides information on the benefits and features of a product, product testimonials. Designed to get contact information or generate sales.

Share - Telling your *story* or providing a *prospect* with a *tool.*

Social Media - Information sharing websites that are used to develop contacts and build relationships.

Sponsor - Enrolling another person in a *network marketing* company. The person who enrolls you is also called your sponsor.

Squeeze Page - A webpage that contains interesting information. Used to attract readers to a certain topic and obtain the reader's name, email address and other contact information. Marketers use this information to promote products at a later date.

Story - A passionate account of your personal product and/or business experience with the company.

TEAM - All of the people connected to the same compensation leg as you, including those above and below you. Acronym for: Together Everyone Achieves More.

Time Freedom - Having sufficient wealth to do the things you enjoy and desire. Being able to manage your own schedule and priorities.

Tools - Information used to introduce and recruit people into your business. Includes your *story,* videos, audios, brochures, business cards.

Upline - The people in your networking organization above you in your *compensation plan.*

Your Why - The compelling reason you do what you do.

40/40 Plan - Slang for 40 hours a week for 40 years.

About the Author

As a successful, mid-life network marketer and mentor, Linda is committed to helping others live life without fear, honor their passion and begin living their dreams more fully. Despite today's faltering economy, there are viable options and exciting opportunities.

Linda has a BA in Philosophy; a Master's degree in Gerontology; and a Master of Divinity degree. She was ordained in the Presbyterian Church (USA) in 1987. She has 30 years combined, professional experience in multinational corporate management (home healthcare & hospital staffing); non-profit leadership; the Interfaith movement; and philanthropy.
Among her passions are network marketing
and mentoring; photography; hiking; writing; playing with her puppies; gardening; and exploring the great Southwest.

Contact the Author

Your feedback and questions are always welcome.

Email: wheycoolhealthstyle@gmail.com

All photographs and images by Linda Compton, all rights reserved. You can find more of her work at http://www.highdesertvisions.com

Made in the USA
San Bernardino, CA
03 April 2015